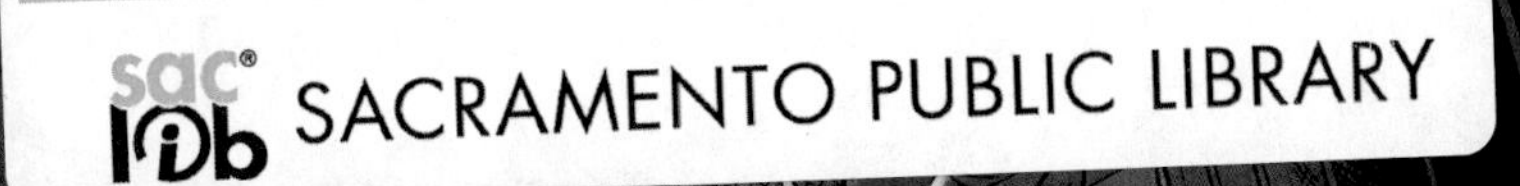

COLLECTION EDITOR **JENNIFER GRÜNWALD**
ASSOCIATE MANAGING EDITOR **KATERI WOODY**
VP PRODUCTION & SPECIAL PROJECTS **JEFF YOUNGQUIST**

**CAITLIN O'CONNELL** ASSISTANT EDITOR
**MARK D. BEAZLEY** EDITOR, SPECIAL PROJECTS
**JAY BOWEN** BOOK DESIGNER

SVP PRINT, SALES & MARKETING **DAVID GABRIEL**
EDITOR IN CHIEF **C.B. CEBULSKI**
PRESIDENT **DAN BUCKLEY**

**SVEN LARSEN** DIRECTOR, LICENSED PUBLISHING
**JOE QUESADA** CHIEF CREATIVE OFFICER
**ALAN FINE** EXECUTIVE PRODUCER

**MS. MARVEL BY SALADIN AHMED VOL. 1: DESTINED.** Contains material originally published in magazine form as MAGNIFICENT MS. MARVEL #1-6. First printing 2019. ISBN 978-1-302-91829-3. Published by MARVEL WORLDWIDE, INC., a subsidiary of MARVEL ENTERTAINMENT, LLC. OFFICE OF PUBLICATION: 135 West 50th Street, New York, NY 10020.  **Printed in Canada.** DAN BUCKLEY, President, Marvel Entertainment; JOHN NEE, Publisher; JOE QUESADA, Chief Creative Officer; TOM BREVOORT, SVP of Publishing; DAVID BOGART, Associate Publisher & SVP of Talent Affairs; DAVID GABRIEL, SVP of Sales & Marketing, Publishing; JEFF YOUNGQUIST, VP of Production & Special Projects; DAN CARR, Executive Director of Publishing Technology; ALEX MORALES, Director of Publishing Operations; DAN EDINGTON, Managing Editor; SUSAN CRESPI, Production Manager; STAN LEE, Chairman Emeritus. For information regarding advertising in Marvel Comics or on Marvel.com, please contact Vit DeBellis, Custom Solutions & Integrated Advertising Manager, at vdebellis@marvel.com. For Marvel subscription inquiries, please call 888-511-5480. **Manufactured between 8/23/2019 and 9/24/2019 by SOLISCO PRINTERS, SCOTT, QC, CANADA.**

10 9 8 7 6 5 4 3 2 1

WHEN A STRANGE TERRIGEN MIST DESCENDED UPON JERSEY CITY, KAMALA KHAN WAS IMBUED WITH POLYMORPH POWERS. USING HER NEW ABILITIES TO FIGHT EVIL AND PROTECT JERSEY CITY, SHE BECAME...

# MS. MARVEL

## Destined


WRITER | SALADIN AHMED
PENCILER | MINKYU JUNG
INKER | JUAN VLASCO WITH MINKYU JUNG (#5-6)
COLORIST | IAN HERRING
LETTERER | VC's JOE CARAMAGNA

COVER ART | EDUARD PETROVICH

ASSISTANT EDITOR | SHANNON ANDREWS BALLESTEROS
EDITOR | ALANNA SMITH
CONSULTING EDITOR | SANA AMANAT

1

OTHER WORLD.
FAR FUTURE.
Tell me again, Father. Tell me about the *Destined One.*
It is time for you to sleep, child.
Pleeeease, Father? Just once more? Tell me the story of how the Destined One came to our world!
Very well, but after this telling, you are going straight to sleep!
YAY!
The Destined One was born long, long ago, on a strange and distant world called *Earth.*
She was that planet's greatest hero. And they called her...

MS. MARVEL!
Foolish girl, you can never defeat Deathbringer! Surrender now or be destroyed!
You're joking, right?
GROVE ST
GROCERY
DELI
FRESH MEATS

e Destined One was known and wide on her world for valor. Her fists were like ulders, her eyes like fire.
You *sure* you want to do this?
"Her spirit was fearless and her manner was bold.
Oh crap!
"Some say the Destined One could shrink out of her enemies' sight.
Huh?
"Some say she could grow to the size of a giant.
Over here, jerky!
ATM
D
You should have stayed out of Jersey City, homicidal goth guy.

"Noble she was in bearing, and solemn in spirit.
Oh, GROSS! It smells like a dead fish ate poop then threw it up! Please tell me you give up so we can get away from this stink.
Unnnh.
Deathbringer yields...
LIQUOR
Thanks for the help, Ms. Marvel!
Don't mention it, Officer. All in day's--
Are you kidding me?
You gonna just walk away after that?!
Oh, no need to thank me. Saving lives is just--
Saving lives?! You trashed my store! What's wrong with you?
I was gonna help clean up, you don't have to yell at me!
"The Destine was belove celebrated the people world.

And she was always a true and steadfast friend.
HABIBI RAW JUICES & SPICES MADE WITH ♥
Nakia!
Where you at?
Over here.
Sorry I'm a little late. There was a crazy guy with a sword who... you know what, never mind.
I'm used to adding 30 minutes for brown people time, but when you add super hero time to that, it's kind of ridiculous.
Keep your voice down! I said I was sorry!
It's fine. I've been hate-watching the hipsters flocking to this new Lebanese juice bar.
feel like they just started building 's place last week. ings are changing so fast downtown...
h-huh.
So this was supposed to be the day you finally tell me all about how you became...you know who.
How have I not told you that story?
Life gets busy when you're an international role model. I understand you don't have time for the little people.
Ha ha ha. Let's take a walk, huh?

It seems so long ago... and also like it was just yesterday.
I was leaving this nasty waterfront party that I should never have gone to.
Kamala the rebel. Nobody understands her. I remember *that* phase.
I stumbled into the Terrigen Cloud that unlocked my powers and thought it was smog from some nearby factory. The first time I started to polymorph, I thought I was drunk.
Well, you *are* a notorious lush.
You're hilarious.
VIDEO
SALE 20%
Did you know the first thing I did as Ms. Marvel was save Zoe from drowning? This is back when I *hated* her.
To be fair, our Zoe was pretty hateable back in the day.
Do you remember how much *you* hated *Ms. Marvel* at first?
I did not!
Rocket
You *so* did. "If Ms. Marvel is only here to profit off the destruction of the city she claims to represent, then she needs to *go*" were your exact words.
Before you knew she was me, obviously.
Oof.

Who did you tell first, as if I can't guess?
Bruno.
Big surprise. And then you told your family.
Much later. And just my Ammi. We thought we were facing the end of the world and I didn't want to go to God with a lie as the last thing in my book.
How *are* things at home, anyway? I hate that we don't have any classes together. Yesterday was the first day of school and I didn't even *see* you.
*Home!* Oh crap. I was supposed to be back there ten minutes ago!
Better get your butt moving, then.
I'm sorry I hogged the conversation. I'll see you Monday!
"Wherever she traveled, the Destined One brought harmony and happiness.
Ammi? Abu?

"And at home, the Destined One always honored her distinguished kin and clan.
We're here, beta.
And we need to talk.
What is it?
*What?!* Why are you guys acting so weird?
Today, beta, I found out some terrible things.
But the worst is that you have been *lying* to me.
Oh no. Oh no no no no no.

Yes, Kamala. I know. About your double life. About *Ms. Marvel.*
*You* told him, Ammi! You *betrayed* me!
*Betrayed?* How long have I kept your secrets? How long have you asked me to live with being a *liar?*
That's a *horrible* way to put it! I never--
*Listen* to yourself. Scolding your own mother! Because she wouldn't *lie* to me? Who have you *become?*
I've become a *hero.*
sorry I kept this from you. I ly am. But I just...I didn't think would understand. I knew you'd *ure* me about how *dangerous* is. And I've helped *so many people,* Abu!
I know. And it does not surprise me that you would use your power to help others. You've always had such a giving heart. Since you were tiny.
But there is such a thing as giving too much. I have seen the news clips. How many times have you almost died?
A...a few. But I've done okay so far.

But it only takes one mistake, beta.
You are only a teenager. You still have your whole life to live. We...I need to protect you. Even if you have super-powers, I'm still your father.
W-what are you saying?
once. As a baby. You almost never got sick. Now I know it's because you are special.
But once, just once, you got so sick and coughed so much I thought you might die. Your mother was away and I had to take care of you and I prayed and prayed and I thought I would die from the sounds coming from your little body...
That's not me anymore, Abu. I'm not a baby.
No. But you are still a girl, however close to a woman you've become. You are still our girl.
This...this parading around God-alone-knows-where in a costume, trying to get yourself killed--it is over. As of tonight.
WHAT?! You can't do this!
Ammi, why did you tell him?! Why now?
You don't understand. Things have changed, beta. Your father is--he's--
That's enough! While you live in our house you will follow our rules. Whether you understand it or not, we must protect you. What would we be if we didn't? Monsters.
You know, I'm not the only one in this family who's been hiding things!
What is that supposed to mean?

Always did the Destined One hold her head high, an inspiration to all.
BZZT BZZT BZZT
Bruno
911 @ Circle Q
what's wrong
MONSTERS.
OMW
I'M GOING TO THE CIRCLE Q!
No, you are not! We're not done talking about--
Bruno's in trouble. You two can be mad at me *after* I save my friend.
Kamala, please, listen. There are things we need to talk about. You can't just--
I *can,* Abu. I *have* to.
And you can't stop me.

GRRRAAAAAAKKKKKK
"No marauding beast was safe when the Destined One took up arms...
Kama--er, *Ms. Marvel!* Am I glad to see you!
Bruno! What the hell *is* that thing?
I was working my shift here and the extraterrestrial threat detector I'd been rigging up for Jersey City started going nuts. Next thing I know *this* slobbering wolf monster drops out of the sky!

Extraterrestrial threat detector?
Yeah. I built it when I was studying in Wakanda. Been tweaking it in between ringing up smushees since I've been back.
Hey, are you okay? Have you been... crying?
What? No!
You *have* been crying--and we still haven't talked about...*uh*...what happened yesterday.
Little busy here, Bruno!
IRCLE
So we're just going to pretend yesterday didn't happen?
*Later* okay?

Yuck. Is it dead?
I...I didn't throw it *that* hard!
The real question is where it--
BEEP! BEEP! BEEP!
Uh-oh.
The waterfront.
Got it.
MINUTES LATER...
GRAAAKKKK!
Well, hey there! I don't suppose this is one of those classic sci-fi moments where you really don't mean Earth any harm and what we have is a tragic miscommuni--
Didn't think so.

ZZZAPPP
Get to safety, all of you! I'll handle this!
OWWWWW!
GRAK? ?
GRAAAAKKK!
ZZZZAAAPPPP
Hey, beaky...

...I'm over here.

Again?! This is so gross it's almost cool.
GURGLE
GURGLE

...Almost.
Something's wrong here. I mean, wronger tha just an alien invasic The cellular structu of these things is...

BEEP! BEEP!
Oh, great, another one.
Oh no.
What is it?
The last signal. It's coming from...
My house.
I have to go, Bruno.
Kamala!
Be careful.

WINES
LOST
24/7
COIN LAUNDRY
Come on... pick up.
Neither of them are answering. Oh God. Oh God, I was so snotty to them. Please let them be safe.
CARE
KARAOKE
"Never did the Destined One falter or fear...
Ammi! Abu!
Abu! Ammi?

What is wrong, beta? Why all this noise?
WAAAAA!
Where did you come from?
Come from? This is our home.
AAAAGHH!
Stop jumping out at me!
Is something wrong?
No. No, nothing's wrong. I... I thought something happened. I thought you were in...
...danger.
"...but then, one day, the Destined One found...

"...that everything had changed."

Wel ome to
JERSEY

Let me tell you about Kamala Khan, my favorite person in the world.
(Don't tell my nonna I said that).
ABU! AMMI!? WHAT'S HAPPENING?!
We've known each other since the second grade.
No no no no! What *is* this?

And if I know one thing about Kamala, it's that she can bounce back from...
I got here as fast as I could! Are the aliens--
...anything?
Oh my God...
What is this, Bruno? **WHAT HAPPENED TO MY PARENTS?**
Oh God. Mr. Khan. Mrs. Khan. They're just--they--
Bruno, I need you to keep it together right now. I need your *help.*
Keep it together. Keep it together. Okay.

Kamala's always been stronger than me. Always struggled to her feet when I'd have stayed down.
I swear, she was *destined* to become a super hero.
According to these readings, the pattern of cellula degradation here is the same as the two aliens you just fought.
This is your parents' genetic material, but... something's off. I wonder if--
I can't believe they're dead, Bruno. I *won't* believe it!
But like any hero, sometimes she needs help *staying* on her feet.
Then they're alive. Whatever's going on, we'll figure it out.
That's what *I'm* here for.
I guess we should start at the Circle Q.

CIRCLE Q
Looks like the cops are already done here. Guess they're getting more used to alien monsters in JC. Used to be a big deal.
That's my fault. Just like my parents--
oa, there. We don't ow what's happened your folks. Let's take this one step at a time.
So what are we looking for?
I wish I knew for sure. I'm trying to find something here to make sense of... uh...what we saw at your house. An energy signature or cellular residue or anything that might--
LINE
O-M-G. Ms. Marvel?! Is that you? You are so awesome! Would you mind if I took a selfie with you? It will--
POLICE LINE DO NOT CROSS
LEAVE ME ALONE!

Uhhh, maybe you should--
SAVE IT!
POLICE LINE DO NOT CROSS
Sorry. I'm just--
Hey, do you... Could this have anything to do with what we saw yesterday?
I...I can't *believe* you're bringing that up now.
You're right. *You're right!* I said I wouldn't mention it again. I just--

Please, Bruno. I can't even think about that. Just help me find my parents.
Already on it. But I need another set of readings for comparison.
POLICE LINE DO NOT CROSS
We could go back to the waterfront. That's where the other creature attacked.
Good idea.
MARKET
POLICE LINE DO NOT CROSS
Bruno? Thanks for being here. Just... thank you.
"Thank you," my favorite person in the world says to me. It feels weird to hear.
You don't need to *thank* me. You ***never*** need to thank me.
We're beyond that. After all these years, she should know that that's just us.
This is getting awkward, isn't it?
Totally. Let's go.

Jersey City Waterfront. Fifteen Minutes Later.
Okay, this is the spot.
I was so mad. I yelled at them that I could handle any threat that came my way. But I couldn't even save them.
POLICE
CROSS
And now they're gone. Maybe dead.
STOP! They're gone. But they're not dead.
POLICE LINE DO NOT CROSS
These readings confirm the monsters were some sort of constructs. Whoever made them also made those freaky copies of your parents.

If they're not dead...that means someone kidnapped my parents. Someone who knows my identity.
Someone's doing this to them to hurt me.
It's my fault that--
Dude, come on. Feel guilty later. Find your Abu and Ahh-mi now.
Um-mi. You always sound so goofy trying to--waitaminute! look!
POLICE LINE DO NOT CROSS
That rooftop! Meet you up there!
Wait!
POLICE LINE DO NOT CROSS
You just failed your stealth check, pal. Now, who--
Shut the front door!

Ms. Marvel!
Discord! W-what are you doing back in Jersey City, Josh? Aren't you a fugitive?
Yeah, Kamala, I am. After you made me one.
I'm sorry, but you went from being my friend from trig class to a fascist super villain. I didn't have a lot of choices.
You were never my friend. But who cares? I've got new friends. Powerful friends. And now I'm gonna kick your--

I don't know what you're talking about, but I'm *glad* you found me, Kamala. Now I can pay you back for ruining my life.
nough
his crap!
ere *are*
hey?
Josh, you *chose* this path. I'm *really* sorry things have been so hard, but that doesn't give you the right to--
P-CHEW!
P-CHEW!
UNH!
Oh, shut up.
I don't *really* want to kill you, Kamala. Why don't you just walk a--

WHERE ARE MY PARENTS?!

Wait, your parents? Something happened to Mr. and Mrs. Khan?
~huff~ ~huff~ I'm here, Ms. Marvel! What did--Josh!
Bruno? I... Kamala said something about her parents being in trouble? Look, you guys, I swear...I don't know anything about that.
LIAR!
I dunno, his vitals say he's telling the truth. But what the hell are you doing up here, Josh?
I'm working. For people who are taking care of me.
Working as in, like, a henchman?
Let me tell you about Kamala Khan. She tries to help everyone. Even people who've tried to kill her.
Josh, look, I had no idea that things were this bad for you. Maybe I can--
Hey! A new alien signal-- a huge one way the hell out in Morristown.
ping! ping!
Abu and Ammi could be there! We'll finish this another time, Josh.
Uh, take care of yourself, okay, man?
Yeah... yeah, sure.

Morristown Municipal airport.
That took forever!
Dude, just be happy my Uncle Angelo let us borrow his van. You have no idea how much convincing that took.
Why is no one here?
Closed for a year. They're doing a total renovation.
Why do you know that?
Mike--one of her cousins worked here. Got laid off right before she and I broke up.
How are you doing with that? Life after--
GRAAAAAAAKKKKK!
K-Kamala, what the hell was that and where did it come from?
My best guess...
...is that THAT--

--is the *final boss* battle.

GRAAAAAAAAAKK!
Yeah, yeah, yeah.
How about less *graaking*--
--and more--
BAM
--handing over my *parents?*
HEY!
SLURK

This thing's hide is too tough.
THLURP!
THLURP!
Gonna have to try something else.
THLURP!
Can't believe I'm doing this...
So. Nasty.

KA-BOOM!
GURGLE GURGLE GURGLE
The melting again? Oh, come--
Huh?
Bruno! There's something inside the--
What the--

Kamala is a *hero*. I've seen her save ersey City, watched er save the earth.
Ammi! Abu!
K-Kamala?
What... what is this?
Oh my God. Oh God, I'm so glad you're okay. I'm so sorry this happened. I love you both *so much.*
Such goodness! Do you see?
She fulfills the foretold signs!
Who in the--

It is time we revealed ourselves.
You're behind this? You're the ones who've been attacking my city? Who kidnapped my parents?
Give me one reason I shouldn't pound you to paste.
She tests us! Stand fast! Long have I watched her! She is mighty but righteous and will not smite those who serve her!
Behold! She stays her smiting hand!
Is it not as I said? Just as it was written, she has been revealed! Sword of Saffa! Shield to a Million Children!
WHO ARE YOU PEOPLE AND WHAT THE FREAKING HELL ARE YOU TALKING ABOUT?!
Do you not understand? With courage you faced the Beast Legions and vanquished them. With goodness you spared the innocent. And with brilliance you tracked us here.
You have the Three Qualities. You wear the Sigil and the Shape!

if I've learned one thing
om growing up and living
d fighting alongside her
all these years...
...it's that she was meant for something. Something **big.**
**You** are **the Destined One!** And it has been written that you will return with us to live on our world, or our planet will **die.**

3
Petrovich

MUNICIPAL AIRPORT.
You have shown courage and brilliance and odness. You wear the shape and display the sigil.
You are the Sword of Saffa, the Shield to a Million Children--you are *the Destined One!*
There was always something different about you. From the moment you were born. The way you locked eyes with me.
What the heck are you talking about?! Who **are** you people?
Uh... **are** you people?
These guys are definitely of extraterrestrial origin. Unknown species. Pretty close to human anatomy, though.
Aliens? My daughter is being harassed by *aliens?!*
You terrified me as a toddler--the way you always seemed to find danger.

Knives, electrical outlets, steep stairways--always exploring, even when I feared it might kill you.
Aliens. Ya Allah.
I don't understand any of this, and I won't pretend to. But if you don't leave our daughter alone, so help me God...
Even now, you think we restrict you. Limit you. You don't understand how proud we are. How much we trust you.
I've got this, Abu.
But part of me will always be young mother who grabbed you you reached for the hot stove.
We mean no harm! Your world is in no true peril--the beasts were mere constructs. We meant only to test. To reveal the Destined One.
And we have revealed her!
But your fear, this destruction, is only a fraction of what awaits our people. If you do not return with us, our whole world is doomed!

Look, I don't know who you weirdos are, but you just attacked my city. You kidnapped my *family*. I'm not ***destined*** to do anything except take you to jail!
Jail? *Uhh*, Kamala, these guys aren't ***burglars***.
Well, we have to do ***something!***
May we show you something, Sword of Saffa?
This is Ayla. She is my grandchild. She knows all there is to know about the care and feeding of sandwrigglers.
This is Ayla's study pod. Each child is bright and loving in their own way.

This is what will happen to them if we face the Beast Legions without the Destined One leading us. It has been foretold.
Without you, Shield of a Million Children, we are doomed. Help us! You are our--
"Only hope." Yeah, I saw that movie.
You've always used your fearlessness to help other people. Since you were very small.
Please, there is little time. We--
My daughter is not going to fight in outer space!
Hey, I'm right here!
What sort of father would send his daughter away with strange men?! No! I forbid it!
Distinguished Father of the Destined One, our families--they will die.
When I learned you had become a super hero, I was not surprised.
Abu, I... maybe I'm supposed to go.

fact, it made
rfect sense.
What?! These guys just attacked Jersey City and now you're gonna go on a road trip into space with them?!
They'll be slaughtered without me, Bruno. So will their kids and grandkids. If I can save a whole planet, I have to try.
And now...
You most certainly do not! I just watched you grow ten feet tall. I haven't even had time to ask you how. Now you want to--
Abu, I love you more than anything. But you have to understand--
...we will find a way to live with it. Together.
Ach! "Understand!" He will never stand by and understand his choti Kamala putting herself in harm's way!
And you will never stop her from putting herself in harm's way. Our daughter has become a hero. She won't walk away from that.
There is only one solution...
Your father and I will come with you to outer space!

That's a *terrible* idea!
The Destined One has accepted her duty, and her honored parents stand by her side!
We will depart...
WAIT!
...NOW!

Well, that wasn't so...
...bad?
Behold, by the grace of our Rightly Ruling King, a feast worthy of welcoming The Destined One!
You could always make us laugh when you were little. You could make a joke of anything.
Ah, I, um-- hi? Is all this for me? A banquet?
I, uh, haven't brushed my teeth in two days.

The Destined One needs no adornment to be a blessed sight before our eyes!

*I scolded you for it sometimes, but I hope to God that you never lose that.*

I am called Maliq Zeer. Seen by the seers and foretold by the scrolls. I am the rightful ruler of this world.

For years, our sages have sought the Destined One on distant worlds. Now, at last, they have found you!
OMG, these smell *amazing!*

Another planet, *jaan.*
I've seen aliens on television. But this...to ***be*** here...
Do you think any of this is *halal*...?

Is this ***normal*** for you, beta? For your... hobby?

Being a super hero is not a ***hobby!*** And no, this isn't ***normal***.

But mostly it's just weird having you two here.

Waitaminute. Where's Bruno? My friend who was with us?
He remains on your world, Sword of Saffa.
Oh...and what about your friend with the eye patch?
All your questions will be answered, Destined One. But first--*behold* the world you will save!
Behold... resplendent **SAFFA!**

Your cheer, your goodness, your boldness--maybe you were destined by God to protect others.
Kamala, this is madness. They are treating you like a Nabi. You are not an alien savior--you're from New Jersey.
They seem pretty sure, Abu.
But whether you like it or not, beta, I was destined to protect you.
Enough, space people. Why do you keep calling our daughter "Destined One"?
Right! Left! My noble sages. I am sorry that your brother could not return with you. His sacrifice will not be forgotten. But I think now it is time for the telling of the tale.
Of course, Honored Mother.
Sacrifice?
As the Rightful Ruler commands!
The sages have set down this story, and now we share it with those who will hear.

affa is our world, ough none know ho named it.
Our home is a place of peace and blessed beauty. But it was not always so.
nce our people were enslaved. nce our lot in life was to toil t the Great Machine for the nseen Masters.
No Saffan knew the purpose of the Great Machine. But we died by the thousands to build it. For centuries, we lived in chains.
ever did we meet our nseen Masters. Only the east Legions--madly bred ings with no minds. We ed beneath their lashes. ur songs seared the heart.
But then the Destined One appeared.

None knew whence she came. But like the lightning made flesh, she blasted the Beast Legions.
Where she struck, they scattered. The Beast Legions left Saffa licking their wounds. The Great Machine rumbled and died.
As quickly as she came, she was gone. Yet she promised to watch over Saffa.
And O, Saffa has prospered since. The wayward forget the Beast Legions of the Unseen Masters.
Ye who read these words--heed the seers and the scrolls. Never forget that our oppressors will return!
Yet you will not face their claws and cannons alone. Know that the Destined One will return also.

nd now
e have
nd her!
And sometimes it is a mother's job...
Would that our brother Center could see this!
He sacrificed himself--burned away his own essence to bring us here. But oh how he would smile tonight!
He what?
...to protect her children from themselves.
This isn't right.
Beta, tell them there's been some mistake.
Hey! How can you guys be so sure I'm not their chosen one? One of them died to bring me here! There has to be something to--
My blessed people! This claimant wears the shape and bears the sigil! I judge her qualities true!
The sigil? Are you talking about my costume? I guess it does look like--
KRASH
NOOOOOOOO!
The antechamber!

Papa! Help! It hurts!
Aqil!
I'm coming!
Let me see if I can help.
The Destined One!
Get while the getting's good, little guy!
Amazing. You are truly Shield to a Million Children!
Another column collapse.
This sabotage has all the hallmarks of Cheb Hura's rebels, O Rightful Ruler.
And yet such treachery cannot stand before our new champion! Spread the word, for her deeds have ratified our judgment--
--the Destined One has returned!
ALL HAIL THE DESTINED ONE!
Sometimes protec
you from yourself..

harder than protecting from the world.
Here are the chambers of the Destined One, the finest in the palace--save those of Maliq Zeer himself, of course.
And where are *we* to sleep?
The Destined One's honored parents will be pleased to note that there are adjoining attendants' chambers, so that you can always be near to minister to the Sword of Saffa's needs!
Tch!
Tomorrow, Destined One, Maliq Zeer will summon you to discuss defending Saffa. For now, I take my leave of you-- rest well!
THIS BED SMELLS LIKE GINGERBREAD AND HUGS!
t even when s hard...
Kamala, we have to leave this place.
What?!
...it must be done.
This attention is going to your head. You're not thinking straight.
Th-that's not true!
I...I just need to get some sleep-- on one of the *little* beds!
Because I'm so *humble!*

Hours Later...
Brain braining too hard. Can't sleep.
Maybe a walk will help.
ZZZZZZZZZZ!
Probably better not to wake them...
Now to just get a breath of--
Huh?
The Destined One still slumbers?
Yes, sir. And the chamber is sonically sealed. We've made certain the prisoner's cries won't disturb her.
Prisoner?

Time for the great *Hope of the People* to get his daily dose of shock stick!
How does that feel, *traitor*?
ZZZAAAPPP!
ZZZAAAPPP!
Give him a moment between jolts, my friends. We want to give him the chance to reveal his fellow traitors' location.
Unnnnh... *never!*
Guys, I don't know a lot about this world...
...but I know assaulting a chained-up person with a cattle prod is *not okay,* whatever planet you're on!
Unnnhh!
BAM!
The Sword of Saffa! I must inform our Rightful Ruler!

Hey, I'm Ms. Marvel. Are you all right?
CRRRACK!
You are she whom they call the Destined One! My thanks.
I am Cheb Hura. I lead those who refuse Maliq Zeer's iron rule. For weeks I have been held in this stinking cage.
Cheb Hura? Didn't your people sabotage that stone column? A little boy almost died!
That was not our work, I swear it. The code of the Free People forbids such atrocities, just as we forbid torture. Maliq Zeer's men, however...
All is not as it seems here. If you would truly save the people of Saffa, aid me now! I must reach my friends, who think me dead.
You uhhh... look pretty alive to me.
If you do not aid me, Destined One, I may die here tonight. Come with me! See the justness of our cause for yourself.
I... I don't know...
Please, Sword of Saffa! Believe what your own eyes tell you. Don't ally yourself with a man who would do... this.
Okay, but I'm not here alone...

, it is my destiny to protect you.
ether from an ear infection or
gerous men or you yourself...
bu! mi! We ve to go!
What's wrong, Kamala? Why do--
ZZZZ-- wha?!
This Maliq Zeer guy is a torturer and maybe a liar and I don't know what else!
Please, we must be away! There is a place near here where we can commandeer a skycraft.
And who is this shirtless beh maan larka?
I'll explain later, Abu!
This way!
WHAM!
Careful! The skycraft will be...
...guarded.
Unh!
langclangclangclang
The alarm! Everyone in, quickly!
Ah-ah, you sit back here next to me, young lady. Your Abu can sit next to the muscular shirtless man.

And on quiet nights, when I can't sleep...
Hold fast, my friends--the ride will not be gentle!
O Rightful Ruler! The Destined One has gone mad! She's freed the traitor Cheb Hura and--
I am aware.
Gunner. Blow them out of the sky.
...I ask myself...
F-forgive me, R-rightful Ruler, but she is--
Fear not, good soldier. If she is *truly* the Destined One, she will survive this.
Now *fire*.
KA-THOOOOOOOM!
...what I will do when I can't protect you anymore.

4
Petrovich
EDJUBEY

FOR MOST OF MY LIFE, OTHER PEOPLE HAVE TRIED TO TELL ME MY OWN STORY.
ARRRRRGGGHHHH!
Kamala!
WHEN I WAS LITTLE, MY PARENTS TOLD ME ABOUT ALL THE IMPORTANT THINGS I'D DO WHEN I GREW UP.
The skycraft is no more! We're going down!
AT SCHOOL, OTHER KIDS TOLD STORIES ABOUT A GIRL I BARELY RECOGNIZED-- A MADE-UP IDEA OF A GIRL THEY THOUGHT WAS ME.
CRRRRASSSSSHHH!

THEN I BECAME A SUPER HERO. COSTUMED ADVENTURER! SAVING THE WORLD!

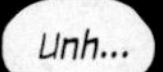
Unh...

AND PEOPLE WERE STILL TELLING ME WHO I WAS SUPPOSED TO BE. INFALLIBLE PROTECTOR. THOUGHT COP. TEAM LEADER.
Abu! Ammi!

BUT THERE COMES A TIME...
Kamala.
I...I'm okay.
Thanks to my little girl.
Thanks to Ms. Marvel.
...WHEN
HAVE TO
YOUR O
STOR

Destined One! You did this? How can I thank you?
Uhhh...yeah, I did. And you don't eed to thank me. But lease stop calling me *Destined One.*
Forgive me. Myth and propaganda. I was raised on stories of you--of *her.* What *shall* I call you?
It's Ka... it's Ms. Marvel.
*Ahem!*

So what now, alien man? How do we get home from here?
TELLING YOUR OWN STORY IS HARDER THAN YOU THINK, THOUGH...
I...I'm not sure we're going home, Abu. Not yet.
WHAT? Of course we're going home. The people who brough us here just trie to kill us!
I'VE BEEN TRYING TO TELL IT FOR YEARS NOW.
The Esteemed Father of the Dest-- of Ms. Marvel--speaks true. Maliq Zeer is a monster. But the people of Saffa are good, and they will die without your aid.
You want us to watch our daughter--a child--fight in your war?
AND SOME DAYS, IT FEELS IMPOSSIBLE NOT TO LET OTHER VOICES DROWN MINE OUT.
We cannot discuss this here. Maliq Zeer's forces will arrive soon to ensure we are dead.
There is a series of tunnels nearby we might use to make our escape. Please, follow me.

These service tunnels extend from the palace throughout the city, far into the countryside. Stay close--they are a labyrinth.
Estimable parents of Ms. Marvel, we warlike types will scout ahead.
SOMETIMES, WHEN HEAD IS ECHOING H EVERYONE ELSE'S ORIES ABOUT ME...
What?! You'll do no such--
Cheb Hura's right. I don't want you two getting hurt.
We're your parents! We--
...I HAVE TO RAISE MY VOICE TO TELL MINE.
PLEASE! I NEED YOU TO TRUST ME!
We will follow you, then, Ms. Marvel.

What's that smell? It's *amazing*.
The perfumigators. They scent the city's wealthy homes. There's an entire set of tunnels for the palace alone. I used to play in them as a child.
As a child?
Indeed. For I was born and raised in the palace. The tyrant Maliq Zeer is my father.
Oh wow. That's... hard.
Don't worry yourself about it, Dest-- Ms. Marvel.
Actually, you can call me Kamala. I guess secret identities don't really matter here. And my father already found out.
He wants me to stop being Ms. Marvel-- to stop saving lives.
He thinks only of your safety-- at least *your* father has not tortured you to learn the location of your rebel base!
You're intense, Cheb Hura.
And yeah, dads...

...really suck sometimes."
So that's it. I'm back in JC for good, and I'm tired of tiptoeing around.
I have feelings for you. I think you have feelings for me. Am I wrong about that?
New Jersey Center For Rare Diseases
You're not wrong, Bruno. This whole summer went by without us seeing each other. I've almost died more than once in the past year. And I keep thinking about what's important to me.
You're important to me.
I think you're the most important thing in the--
OHMYGOD IT'S MY DAD!
What?! Did he follow us?
He...he doesn't see us. Who is that woman he's with?!
Why is she touching him like that?!
Bruno... I...I need to go home.

HELP! PLEASE, SOMEONE!
What was that?
The exit we seek is ahead, but there's some sort of trouble. We must be careful, O Valiant Kamala!
"O Valiant Kamala"?
Shh! We must approach--
PLEASE! SOMEONE STOP THEM!
--quietly?
Sorry, I'm not good at tiptoeing when people are screaming for help!
Please! Stop! I need those coins for food-- Wha--?
Can it be?

Leave him alone!
Who--
Take *that,* brute!
Is that all of them?
'Twould seem so.
*Uhh,* I hope you're not planning on impaling anyone while we're hanging out. I'm... not into that.
Ah, mercy and valor hand in hand in the same soul! 'Tis a rare--
*Kamala!*

Are you all right?!
What happened?
Saved by the Destined One! Just like in the stories! Never did I think I would live to see this day! Thank you! Thank you!
SO YES, SOMETIMES I'VE RAISED MY VOICE
SOMETIMES I'VE HAD TO, TO GET ANYONE TO LISTEN.
I'm from yon village. The people call it Mud Crust. Where Maliq Zeer starves those he is sworn to protect.
And instead of food he gives them armed oppressors. But perhaps you will help change that.
I'm still not sure why I'm here.
Yet you are here. And you are magnificent.
Eerm...
Young man! Behave!

What is that?
The Song of the Stars.
Sages in every village and every city once read it out three times a day for all to hear. Until Maliq Zeer banned it. Whoever's down there singing it is brave.
It's...
...beautiful.
It sounds a lot like the call to prayer back on my planet. Took me by surprise.
Guys, up against the wall!
A palace skycraft--the tyrant's forces are after us. Well spotted.

"We should keep moving."
There! That old well there.
The button is here somewhere... *ah!*
CLICK!
You rebels sure hid your base **well.**
Yes, stealth is--*ah!* I see! "Well"! **HA!**
Someone who appreciates puns!
Do you see this?
I see it.

Your wit is as fierce as your fighting spirit, Valiant Kamala.
How about just "Kamala"?
BUT ONCE IN A WHILE, YOU LEARN PARTS OF YOUR OWN STORY...
...BY LISTENING TO SOMEONE ELSE WHO BELIEVES IN YOU.
I believe you **are** destined to save Saffa--not from the Beast Legions, for they are just an old story for frightening children. But from those among our own people who would--
Intruders? I'll--wait... can it be?
**CHEB HURA!** Blast you, boy, we thought you were dead!
There were times I wished as, *Knuckle*. But free now. Thanks these folks. Good people, this is Knuckle.
We need food and clean water, my friend...

"...and then I need to speak to the Free People."
My friends! Though our fare is meager and our numbers too few, this is a feast of celebration. For the Destined One has come to Saffa, and she stands with the Free People!
Long life to the Destined One!
Valiant Kamala, back on your world--do you have a first-heart?
Whoa, whoa, whoa. A what?
A first-heart. A prime mate. One you have spoken your soul's truths to.
I...uh...like a boyfriend? No That's not...how my life works.
BECAUSE AS IMPORTANT AS IT IS TO TELL YOUR OWN STORY...
I mean, there is someone. Who matters to me. But he and I...a thing happened between us, and...well, it's complicated.
...SOMETIMES YOU JUST NEED TO HEAR THE BEST STORY ANYONE'S EVER TOLD ABOUT YOU.
I am not surprised that one so incredible has claimed her first-heart already. But I would proudly be thy second-heart. You need only command it.
That--that sounds--

CLANG CLANG CLANG CLANG
The alarm!
So that's not the dessert bell?
Maliq Zeer's forces have found us!
To arms! To arms! Honored elders, get the children to the hiding shelters. The rest of you, to your stations!
They will kill us all if they can, then they will enslave the children.
I'm not going to let that happen.
Follow me, then, magnificent one.
Abu! Ammi! Go with the others to the shelter!
Kamala!
We won't go without--
No time to argue! I'll come get you as soon as it's safe!

These traitors have bewitched the Destined One! Crush them all!
Little hint, guys...
If you've got body armor and laser guns...

Behind me, boy!
Nay, old friend. If we die this day, we die side by side!
Hey! Nobody needs to die, okay?!
...and you're hunting down plucky rebels...
...you're probably the bad guys!
Oof!
Okay! That should--

Halt! All of you lay down your arms, or the Esteemed Parents of the Destined One will pay the price.
Kamala!
Don't listen to this monster, beta! He doesn't scare us!
Abu! Ammi! Don't worry, I won't let him hurt you!
I'll do whatever you want! Please just let them go.
In time. You have my word. But first--
Rightful Ruler! Something is amiss!

The orbital detectors, they--oh no.
SO WHEN SOMEONE TELLS YOU A GOOD STORY ABOUT YOURSELF, HOLD ON TO IT.
No.
Ya Allah.
W-what is--
It-- it can't be!

BECAUSE YOU'LL NEED IT WHEN EVERYTHING ELSE GOES WRONG.
The prophecies spoke true. THE BEAST LEGIONS HAVE RETURNED!

OUT of the CHAOS...
...COMES A NEW COSTUME!
Petrovich edjubey

THE PLANET SAFFA. THE FUTURE.
Father, you promised we would finish the story of the Destined One tonight!
Indeed I did! Now where were we? *Ah,* yes...
The Beast Legions darkened the sky. The Destined One faced her final battle, the fate of our world on her shoulders. Yet death could not frighten her...

I KNOW MORE ABOUT DEATH THAN I SHOULD.
The Beast Legions! They have returned!
Abu! Ammi! Get behind me!
Kamala! Muneeba! Get behind me!
I LOOKED UP THE NUMBERS, AND I'VE HAD, LIKE, FIVE HUNDRED TIMES MORE NEAR-DEATH EXPERIENCES THAN THE AVERAGE TEENAGER.
Father, I beg you--let us fight! We must face this threat together or we are all doomed!
I'VE TRIED TO NOT LET IT MAKE ME TOO...GOTH. I'VE LEARNED TO LAUGH AT MY OWN MORTALITY.
Y-yes. Yes, fight beside us. We will need every warrior on Saffa to come to its defense.
SO FACING DEATH DOESN'T MAKE ME MORBID.
BUT IT SURE AS HECK MAKES ME PROTECTIVE.
Stay back and let me handle this!

GRAAAAAAAAAK!
GRAAAAAAAK!
AND I'VE GOTTEN PRETTY GOOD AT PROTECTING WHAT MATTERS.

GRAAAA--
Stay down!
WHAMMM!
PRETTY DARN GOOD AT IT, IF I DO SAY SO MYSELF.
Are you two okay?
There are too many!
Recall the stories I once read to you, Cheb Hura! The Beast Legions are laboratory bred only to kill and die. Even united, our forces will not hold long.

Where can we regroup and mount a defense?
Preferably somewhere on high ground.
You are wise in the ways of war, Destined One.
I led a super hero team...and played a lot of *Battlecraft*.
Your valor has crushed the Beasts who set upon us, Destined One!
Yeah. Great.
'Tis a grim sight. But our young and elderly will have time to hide now--because of you. Five hundred children.
Five hundred children. Do you see this, *jaanu*? Our daughter. Our daughter the ***super hero.***
I see it.
AND WHEN I'M FACING DEATH, IT FEELS ***GOOD*** TO HAVE THE PEOPLE I LOVE RECOGNIZE THAT I'M GOOD AT WHAT I DO.
I ***also*** see this young man's hand on my daughter's shoulder, which he had better remove this instant!
*Heh.*

We will retreat to the royal palace and stage our defense there.
Forgive me, Rightful Ruler, but we cannot. I have received word that the palace has already fallen.
This is the end, then. Saffa dies today. My daughters...
No! There is a way! The Great Machine! We must get the Destined One to the Great Machine!
Absolutely not! All who approach the Great Machine are struck down by its strange power--driven away, driven mad...even slain. We can't ask her to--
BUT THAT RECOGNITION ISN'T WHY I DO IT. THE DAY IT BECOMES THE REASON, I'LL HAVE STOPPED BEING A HERO.
You don't need to ask.

SOON...
Nearly there!
The Great Machine gives off a signal that keeps all from approaching.
If you can resist it, valiant Kamala, you will have to enter alone.
What?! No! That's too--
Abu. I--
I know. I know. You can do this. And...I *believe* you can. I'm so proud of--
ABU!
They've found us! We're going down!
KA-BOOOM!

I am **really** tired of getting shot out of the sky!
Get the Destined One and her family into my skycar!
Everyone inside!
Take the helm, Cheb Hura!
It won't bear us all. And someone must slow these monsters. My son--get the Destined One to the Great Machine. We will buy you the time.
*Father!*
I have been shaped by the wrong things, my son. And none of them matter now. If our world survives, let it be guided by the spirit of the Destined One. Brave. Selfless. Smiling.
Goodbye, father. If only things had been different between us.
We can't just leave them to die! Your father--
Maliq Zeer sacrificed himself to get you to-- **ARGH!**

It's the signal from the Great Machine! It will drive us mad if we go any farther! We must land!
Signal?
Truly? You do not feel this pounding in your skull like war hammers?
I feel it!
Then there can be no doubt. You are the Sword of Saffa--born to wield the Great Machine and once again save our world.
I don't know about being born to do it. But I'll try.
THERE ARE TIMES WHEN THIS LIFE SPENT PROTECTING WHAT MATTERS MAKES YOU FEEL COMPLETELY ALONE.
The Beasts seem to be avoiding the Great Machine, so your Esteemed Parents should be safe here with me...for now.
I have to do this. I hope you understand.
Beta, I don't understand any of this. Other planets. Giant machines. Purple young men without shirts.
I don't understand any of it, either. But--though I forgot it for a while--I trust you. Hero.

BUT WHEN YOU HAVE THE TRUST OF THOSE YOU LOVE--WHEN YOU KNOW THEY'RE ROOTING FOR YOU AS YOU FACE THE UNKNOWN...
...THEN YOU'RE NOT ALONE.
Wowwwww.
BEEP!
BEEP!
Huh?

All Glory to the Empire. This is Kree Stormranger 20-14's Deep Space Sectors report.
Kree? She looks... like me.
The people of this planet call it Saffa. Uncolonized by our noble Empire. I was passing it on my patrol when I noticed anomalous technology on its surface and stopped to investigate.
She's the origina Destined One!
What I found was an automated battle station of unknown origin capable of atomizing ground targets and passin spacecraft. The first stage of an invader's fortress.
The weapon was built using indigenous slave labor, overseen by an army of vicious genetic constructs. The constructs seemed to be guided remotely by an orbiting ship.
Sensing a potential threat to the Empire, I took control of the battle station using my ship's computer and my nanosuit. I used its energy weapons to destroy the invaders and their ship.
HISSSSS
The primitive people of this world have been freed. My surveys find the planet unfit for colonization, but there is the matter of what the people here call the "Great Machine."
I've set a bio-haze field to admit only those of Kree blood. My nanosuit has bonded with the machine, so I'm leaving it here for the next Stormranger. Next I'll--
BIO-HAZE FIELD? IS IT BECAUSE I'M AN INHUMAN THAT THE DEFENSES DIDN'T AFFECT ME? WHY WEREN'T MY PARENTS ABLE TO APPROACH? SO MANY QUESTIONS.

UT PART OF THE REASON 'E BEEN ABLE TO CHEAT EATH IS I'VE LEARNED O BE LESS PARALYZED BY QUESTIONS.
I'VE LEARNED THAT SOMETIMES, IN THE FACE OF CHANGE, YOU JUST HAVE TO...
--BZZZZZZT--
...ADAPT.
Rad!

Okay, so apparently the real Destined One used this suit to interface with the machine.
Here goes nothing...
ARRRRRGHHH!
It hurts so much!
VRNNNNN

That ship... emitting a signal. That's what's controlling the Beast Legions!
No life-forms. Not even a sentient A.I. It's just...an algorithm. A giant remote control on a feedback loop forcing these things to fight.
I can't just blast all these monsters, even if they are constructs. But if I destroy that control ship, maybe I can send them all running home.
BREEEEEEEE!
Space shooters aren't usually my thing, but in this case I'll make an exception!
ARRRRRRGHHH!

The Unseen Masters' ship!
It was the Destined One!
Can it be? They flee!
I *told* you she would save us, Knuckle!
So you did, child. So you did.

HANGE
HARD.
BUT IT'S BETTER THAN DYING. BETTER THAN LETTING OTHER PEOPLE DIE.
Cheb Hura!
Valiant Kamala! You have saved us all! But the Great Machine has taken its toll. May I heal you?
Wow... that feels... mmmm...
WHOA! Whoa, that's enough of that.
Have I done something wrong?
No. Not wrong. I just... I need to get back to my parents.
I'm so sorry about your father.
Do not be. You gave him and me our only pure moments together in years. I only hope you and your father can find peace.
Yeah, me too.

KAMALA!
Are you all right?
You saved their lives, beta. These old people. These children.
Destined One! Destined One!
You can call me Ms. Marvel, buddy!
I wanted to show you-- I'm writing a story about how you saved us!
OMG! ALIEN FANFIC ABOUT ME! I love it, thank you!
You're still wearing the suit.
It's ancient Kree nanotech. And it seems to respond to me.
I think maybe it's time for a change. I'm gonna keep it.

It looks right on you, beta. And as terrifying as this was, I am glad I could be here with you.
Me too. But...*ah*...how are we getting home?
Leave that to me.
Left! You survived!
Aye, my prince. It would seem my old, used-up life was meant to end elsewhere. Here, in fact.
W-what are you talking about?
Destined One, I shall send you and your Esteemed Parents home using the same magic of self-sacrifice that my brother used to **bring** you here. I am the last on Saffa who knows it.
**WHAT?!** No! We'll figure out another way! I'll find some way to call--
It is my **destiny,** Shield to a Million Children. And truth be told, I am happy to do it. I miss my brothers and can think of no nobler passage to the Realm of Tranquility than aiding our world's savior.
*Eh?* Of course, my prince! 'Twould mean but a slight alteration to the spell, and 'twould make a fine gift for the Destined One!
Farewell, valiant Kamala. I think your troubles will be fewer when you return home.
No! Don't do this! I can't ask--
Ah, Destined One...
...you don't have to **ask.**

SOMETIMES YOU THINK YOU CHEAT DEATH.
"Troubles will be fewer"? What does that mean? And--
Waitaminute, I'm home! And wearing the new costume!
I'm gonna have to find a bag to keep it in or--
What the--
Okay, *that's* cool.
But where are--
KNOCK KNOCK!
Abu! Ammi!
Hello, beta.
Sit down, please. We need to talk.
Thank God you're okay! **MY PARENTS SURVIVED THE ALIENS' WORLD WAR!**
Aliens? Kamala, this is not the time for your *paagal* computer games.

Remember, beta?
You... you don't remember?
Wait. Wait. NEITHER of you remembers?
Oh my God. Okay, forget the aliens. Do either of you remember my secret identity?
Identity? Beta, please. This isn't the time for your fanfeek or whatever it is called. Please, sit and listen to your father.
THING IS...
I went to the doctor's the other day, Kamala. The New Jersey Center for Rare Diseases, it is called.
Kamala... beta. I'm sick. And there is no cure.
...SOMETIMES DEATH CHEATS YOU BACK.

6

BEFORE I WAS EVEN BORN, I STOOD OUT. YOU MIGHT SAY I WAS DESTINED TO. MY BLOOD BEARS THE MARK OF ALIEN EXPERIMENTS A HUNDRED THOUSAND YEARS OLD.
I STOOD OUT IN MY FAMILY.
WELCOME TO OUR PARENT-TEACHER CONFERENCES
I STOOD OUT AT SCHOOL.
EVEN AMONG DEMIGODS AND MONSTERS AND PEOPLE IN COSTUMES, I STOOD OUT.
SO WHEN I WENT TO AN ALIEN WORLD AND I STOOD OUT THERE, I WAS READY FOR IT. I SAVED AN ENTIRE PLANET.
NOW I'M HOME AND ALL I WANT TO DO IS SHRIVEL UP AND DISAPPEAR.

I'm *sick,* beta. And there is no cure.
Whoa, whoa, whoa, you *what?*
Is...is this about the super hero thing? About the alien planet? Are you still mad that--
Super hero? What is this nonsense you keep talking about? Your father is trying to tell you something!
A month ago I started having terrible pains. Our doctor sent me to the New Jersey Institute for Rare Diseases downtown.
Abu, no--
It turns out I have a brand-new disease they haven't named yet. Only 30 people in the world have it. I have won a sweepstakes!
It won't take my life next week or next month. But eventually I *will* die from it. No one can cure it.

There's got to be a *mistake.*
It's no mistake, beta.
Dr. Hourani, she is a *genius.* But some things only God can do.
Doctor? The woman I saw you with when Bruno and I--*er*...the woman I saw you with before we fought about the Ms. Marvel thing and took our family trip to planet Saffa!
She was just your *doctor!* I was so stupid! How could I think--
KAMALA!
Planet Saffa? What in the name of God are you going on about?
You really don't remember, do you?

You--you know what? That's not important now. Abu, what can I do for you?
Do you see this brave daughter of ours?
I see her.
Have you told Aamir?
Yes. Your brother and Tyesha will be here this afternoon. Traffic shouldn't be too bad on a Sunday.
Wait, it's still *Sunday?* But we must have been gone a couple *days!*
Who was gone where?
Cheb Hura said my troubles would be fewer when I returned home. I wonder if he somehow--
BZZT

Nakia
studying at the juice bar. Carrelli coming, probs Zoe. come edumacate urself. 🤓
What's going on, beta?
It can wait.
From Nakia?
Go study with your friends! Live! None of you are allowed to turn this house into a graveyard! And me being a little sick is no excuse for your grades to slip!
O-okay. Okay. I'll be back by ten, don't worry.
I always worry about you, Kamala. But I know you will be strong. Every day you make me proud.

HABIBI
RAW JUICES & SPICES MADE WITH ♡
WHEN YOU STAND OUT, YOU'RE NOT ALLOWED TO SHRIVEL UP AND DISAPPEAR. SO YOU GO ON FACING LIFE THE BEST YOU CAN.
KARAOKE
--rare disease. Sorry to bother you but I need help and I'm out of options.
BUT YOU TRY NOT TO DO IT ALONE...
Kamala!
Nakia! Bruno!
You're back from... your trip. Are you okay?
Uh, sort of? A lot has happened in the last like, eight hours. I think magic time manipulation was involved.
In less weird news, I got you an orange-carrot-ginger with extra protein.
Thanks.

You guys remember, right? About my identity, I mean. My mom forgot! And my dad found out and then forgot!
Uh, well, I remember.
Wait, your dad found out? Oh, dude. I bet he lost it!
He did. But I think Cheb Hura had my parents' knowledge of my...other life erased when we were sent back.
Erased?
Stupid alien prince! He probably thought he was helping, but he should have asked. I knew he was too cute to be trusted!
Uh-- who was too cute?
Bruno, I--
Guys? Excuse me, guys?
ARE WE GOING TO STUDY OR NAH?

Nakia! I'm dealing with some *stuff* here. Be a friend!
I *am* being your friend, Kamala. I'm trying to make sure that all your magical space adventures don't keep you from getting into college.
...Of course you are. I'm sorry. You're the freaking best, and I love you.
*Ugh,* we're in the mushy part of the ever already, *huh*? I love you too.
I found out something else today. My dad is sick. Like, no-cure sick.
*What?*
That woman we saw him with the other day? That's his doctor. He has some crazy rare disease.

I'm so sorry, Kamala.
You need some sugar. They have this dessert here with honey and cheese. *Koonaff... Kanoof...*
*Kanafeh.*
Yeah. ***That.*** I know you consume a ton of calories as--
*Ms. Marvel?!*
He's asking for *Ms. Marvel?*

LIVE
Yup. Calls himself Deathbringer. Guess he just broke out of prison. And kidnapped a bus full of people.
He says he'll trade them for Ms. Marvel.
STANDING OUT HAS MADE ME A TARGET TIME AND TIME AGAIN.
Looks like I've got to go, guys.
Be careful, okay?
I DON'T HIDE FROM THAT ANYMORE. I KNOW THERE'S NO SHRINKING AWAY.
It's dangerous to go alone. Take this.
BUT IT'S GOOD TO BE HOME, WHERE MY FRIENDS CAN HELP ME FACE IT.

That darkness...must be Deathbringer's doing. The bus has to be in there. Time to suit up.
I'VE LEARNED THAT PEOPLE WILL TAKE THEIR SHOTS AT ME, WHETHER I'M COWERING OR STANDING TALL.
That is, if I can figure out how this new costume... oh!
It seems to know what it's supposed to do.
I'M WEARING A BULL'S-EYE NO MATTER WHAT.
MIGHT AS WELL MAKE IT LOOK COOL.

Deathbringer! I'm here!
I can't see anything, but I'm here! Let those people go.
So is the name "Deathbringer" from your mom's side or your dad's?
Please just let those people go.

Such weak
rks mean little to me,
Marvel. My shadows
not feed on weakness
urrender. Deathbringer
ere to smother *your*
bright light.
*Smother?* Gross. Also, don't you need your Uzi and your cool-guy katana or whatever?
Foolish girl. You last faced Deathbringer in the accursed daylight hours, when he must hide behind men's tools. But now it is night. Now it is the new moon. And now my arcane power...

...RISES!
You have cheated death many times, Ms. Marvel.
Stay back!
But this day--
Back!
--death will have its due!
Hrrrnf!

C-can't embiggen. What are these things *doing* to me?
MY POWERS SEEM TO FAIL ME, AND I WORRY: WHAT IF THIS MANIAC IN A MASK IS RIGHT?
WHAT IF DEATH-- WHAT IF GOD IS JUST TIRED OF ALL MY SKIN-OF-THE-TEETH, LAST-MINUTE RESCUES?
I'M NOT EVEN 18, BUT I'VE LIVED A LOT. WHAT IF I'VE USED UP MY LIVES AND MY GAME IS SUPPOSED TO **END?**
POP!
MY COSTUME! IT'S...HELPING?
SENDING ME IMPRESSIONS...

OF COURSE!
THE MASK IS A CELL THAT STORES SOLAR ENERGY DURING THE DAY AND CREATES THESE THINGS AT NIGHT.
TECH, NOT MAGIC. I CAN USE MY SUIT TO FIGHT IT.
NOT ANCIENT JUDGMENT. JUST SOME JERK WITH DEADLY TOYS.
CRUNCH!
I'M NOT BEING SINGLED OUT BY GOD. LIFE IS JUST HARD.
No! No!
Abandoned by the shadow!
Deathbringer... is defeated.

Looks like you saved Jersey City again, Ms. Marvel.
From a threat that was *my* fault.
Hey, now. Evil people are gonna do evil. If it weren't you, that fella would have found some other excuse. We've all got enough blame to take on-- don't go taking on other people's.
Thanks. I think I... needed to hear that.
New costume, *huh?* Kinda flashy, but it works.
WHOOOSH!
*It doesn't just* **work**, *it's* **faaaabulous!**

I got your text. And I brought gyros.
Iron Man!
MS. GYRO
LATER...
...and ~munch~ ~munch~ that was it. Saved a bus full of people, so ~munch~ ~munch~ that's something.
And the new costume? Alien nanotech, *huh?* Adapted Kree technology, if I had to guess. You've been busy, kiddo.
Thought-responsive interface without neural invasion... Light antiballistic capacity... Configurable environmental protections... This thing is sweet!
Tony... about my dad...

Yeah, I've been
that.
It's not good, kiddo.
The disease is still in a very early stage...
...but in its advanced stages, it's terminal.
Is there any treatment?
I've got a lab in Zurich researching a cure, but it's heinously slow work. They'll crack it someday-- but that doesn't help you.
I am so sorry.

I can tell you this: Some of us spend every day of our lives wishing we'd made things right with our parents before they died.
You have some very precious time left with your dad. Decide how you want to spend it.
Thanks, Tony. Really. It means a lot. I...I think I just need to be alone.
I get that. But you know how to reach me if that changes. Anytime, kiddo. I mean that.
EVEN WHEN GOD DOESN'T SINGLE US OUT, PEOPLE DO. SOMETIMES THEY EVEN THINK YOU'RE A HERO. AN EXAMPLE.
BUT RIGHT NOW I'D GIVE JUST ABOUT ANYTHING TO NOT HAVE TO BE MAGNIFICENT.
TO BE CONTINUE

#1 VARIANT BY
**ELSA CHARRETIER & MATTHEW WILSON**

#1 VARIANT BY
**BABS TARR**

#2 VARIANT BY
**AFU CHAN**

CHRACTER DESIGNS BY
**MINKYU JUNG**

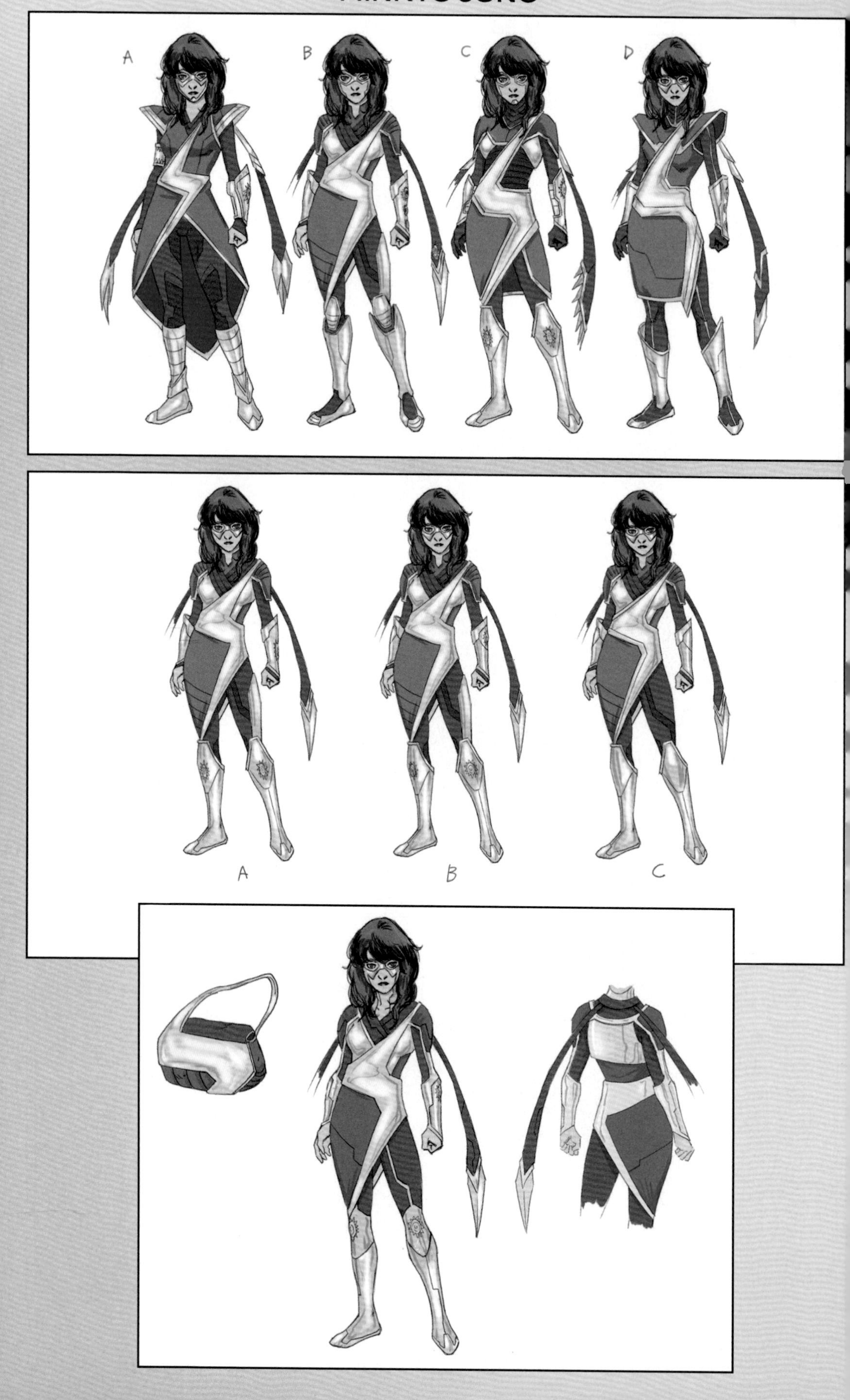

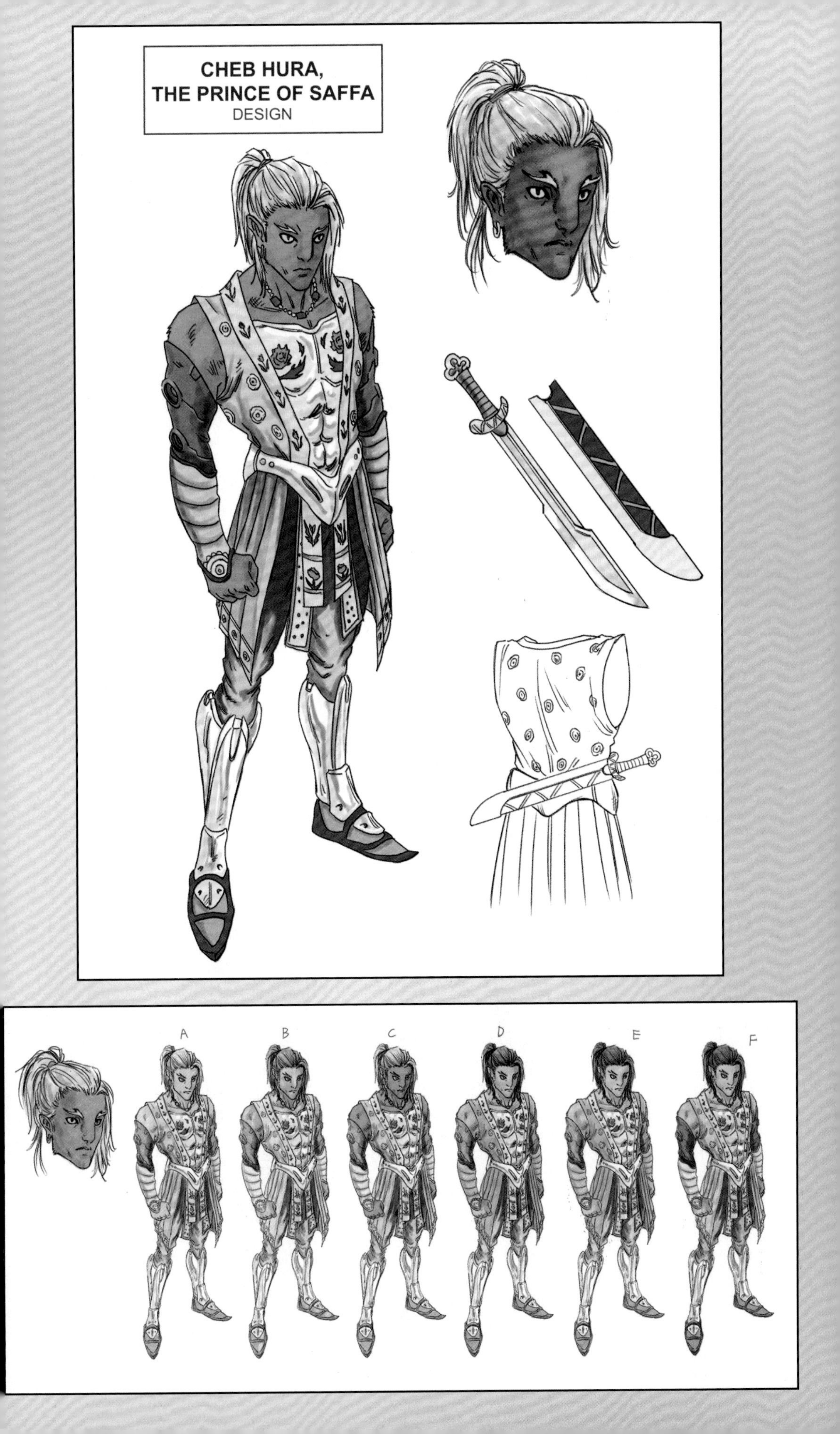
CHEB HURA,
THE PRINCE OF SAFFA
DESIGN
A
B
C
D
E
F

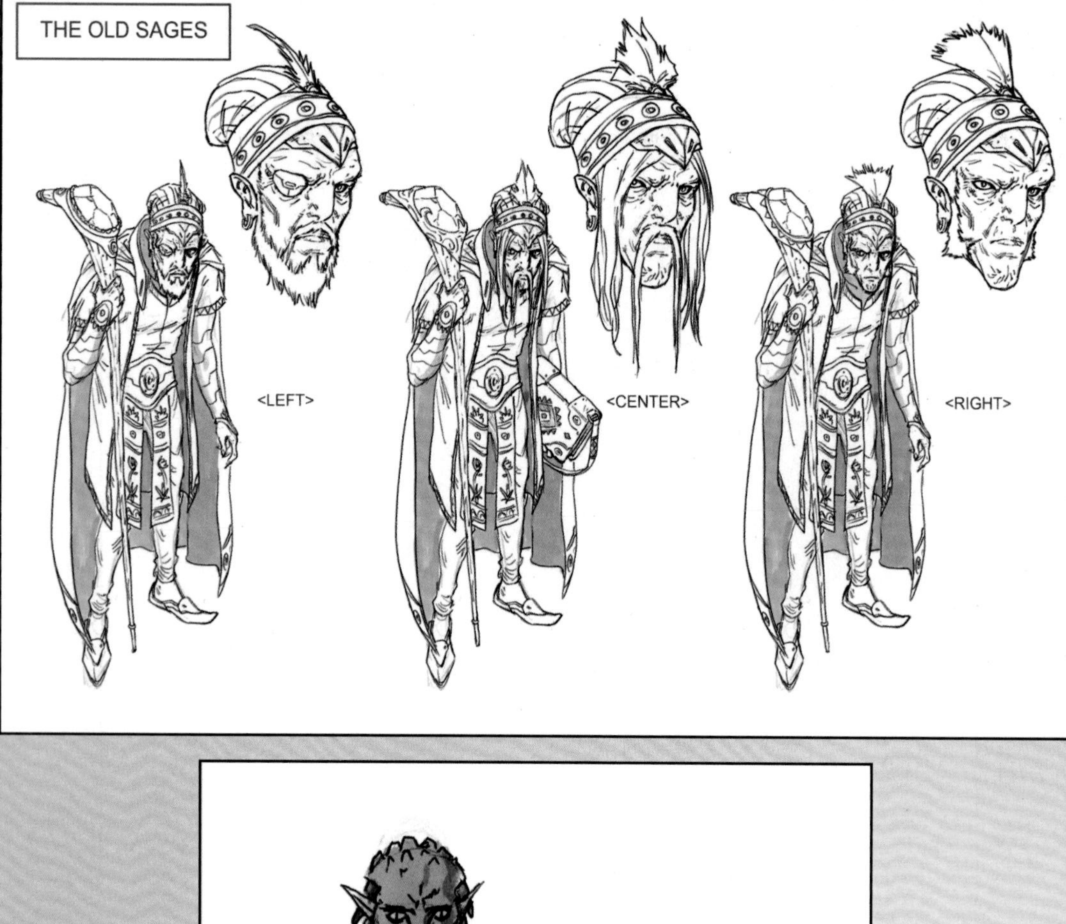
THE OLD SAGES
<LEFT>
<CENTER>
<RIGHT>